THE SPRING PARADE

Cheryl L Jordan

Published by Wagging Tales Publishing

"Spring is here;
spring is here;
spring is here!"
chimed the excited bunnies.

It's time for the spring parade.

Who's ready for the spring parade?

Me.

Me.

Me.

"I am!"
croaked frog bunny.

"Me too!"
chirped duck bunny.

It's so much fun.
Eggs everywhere.

Eggs in trees.

In bushes,
on bushes,

and
behind
bushes.

Look up,
what do you see?

The most perfect
eggs anyone
ever did see.

Look over there,
what do you see?

One perfectly
happy bunny!

The bunnies hunt here, there, and everywhere all day long.

When the
hunt is done,

they are done, too.

The bunnies love
the spring parade.

www.ingramcontent.com/pod-product-compliance
Lightning Source LLC
Chambersburg PA
CBHW042113040426

42448CB00002B/260